Making Mummy Better

Making Mummy Better

A child's experience of post natal depression

Denise Scott

SPECTRUM PUBLICATIONS 2001

First published in Australia in 2001

by Spectrum Publications Pty Ltd

PO Box 75, Richmond, Vic, 3121

Telephone: +61(13) 00 540 736

Facsimile: + 61(13) 00 540 737

e-mail: spectrum@spectrumpublications.com.au

website: www.spectrumpublications.com.au

Artwork: Steven Hallam

Cover design: Steven Hallam

Typesetting: Spectrum Publications

Typeface: Optima/Joanna MT

ISBN 0 86786 315 3

Dedication

For Sarah and Nicholas
Thankyou for being the wonderful,
loving children that you are
and for helping to
make Mummy better...

Acknowledgements

I wish to acknowledge the support of the ACT Postnatal Depression Support Group over the years, and their commitment to the successful publication of *Making Mummy Better*.

I would like to express my appreciation to the Defence Family Support Funding Program for their generous financial contribution to the publication of the book.

I would also like to acknowledge the support and contribution of ideas for illustrations by Tracey Hull.

Finally, my sincerest thanks to Robyn Roe (community nurse) for helping me on my journey to healing, which made this book possible.

Foreword

When I returned from annual leave and found the manuscript of Making Mummy Better on my desk, I was delighted. This gap has been waiting to be filled for a long time.

Those of us who work with mothers who have experienced anxiety and depression are very aware that everyone in the family is affected by the situation. This is hardly surprising, as the role mothers play is so important. They have been referred to by Professor Myrna Weissman as 'the emotional lynchpin' of the family.

Helping such families is, therefore, not simply a matter of working out strategies for short and longer term management of anxiety and depression in an individual woman (or man, since fathers also may experience these problems). If such a difficult experience is to have a happy ending, one must always consider how all the relationships affected by the distress of the parent may be restored and strengthened. Knowing how to explain the situation to children and to the current baby when she or he is older, is a considerable dilemma and, I regret to say, is usually overlooked. All professionals working in the field of perinatal health will welcome the arrival of this much-needed book with its wonderful complementary illustrations. Both Author and Illustrator are to be congratulated on such a fine product; it will help a great many people.

Bryanne E.W. Barnett M.D., FRANZCP

Professor of Perinatal and Infant Psychiatry,

University of New South Wales.

Sally couldn't sleep. She stared out at the night sky, watching the stars twinkling above. Sally remembered when her mother used to look out at the stars with her and they would sing 'twinkle twinkle little star' together. Then her mother would say 'choose a star Sally and make a wish' - but that was before Ben, her baby brother was born. Sally sighed. So many things had changed since Ben was born. She closed her eyes tight and made a wish. 'I wish I could make my Mummy better'.

Sally wasn't sure what was wrong with her mother. She remembered the day her mum brought Ben home. Everyone was so excited. Sally's nanna was staying with them while her mother was in hospital. Her nanna fussed around all morning, cleaning and telling Sally to tidy up the toys because today was a very special day. Sally's mum walked in holding Ben in her arms. She walked straight over to nanna and gave Ben to her saying, 'I'm very tired, I'm going to have a sleep now.' Sally's dad and nanna seemed surprised and told her mum they would wake her later.

Sally noticed that her mother was always sleepy after Ben was born. She would lie on the sofa with her arm over her eyes and groan every time Ben cried. When Sally asked her mother to play with her, she would say 'not today Sally, I am too tired'. She was always angry too. She would walk about the house with a frown on her face and when Sally asked 'what's wrong mummy', she would say 'go away, not now Sally. Why don't you go and play in your room?'

Sally remembered one day when her mother was sleeping and had told Sally not to wake her. Sally decided to do some painting and tried to get the paints down out of the cupboard herself. She dragged the chair over from the table and standing on tiptoes reached up into the cupboard. Her fingers stretched out around the bottle, but as she pulled it towards her, it slipped from her hand. The bottle tumbled off the shelf, falling to the floor, splotch! Sally's mother woke up with a jolt. She saw the mess and yelled, 'Sally what are you doing?' Then she sat down on the floor and cried.

Sally shivered as she remembered that day. She rushed to get her mother some tissues and said 'I'm sorry Mummy, please don't cry'. But her mother always cried after Ben was born. Sally's Dad said 'don't worry, Mummy is just tired.' After a while even her Dad looked worried. Sally's Mum and Dad started arguing a lot. One night her Mum said to her Dad, 'You just don't understand.' She shouted at Sally 'go to your room' and then Sally heard Ben screaming and Daddy saying 'I'll take care of him, you go and rest.'

The sun shone through Sally's window. She opened her eyes and could hear a strange voice coming from the lounge room. She walked out of her room towards the voice, stopping in the doorway. A lady was sitting next to her mother holding her hand. Her Dad had Ben in his arms and he was quietly rocking him from side to side. The lady smiled at Sally. 'You must be Ben's big sister' she said. 'My name is Rose, I am a nurse.' Sally walked over to her mum and leaned against her. 'Are you going to make my mummy better?' she asked. The nurse said 'Well Sally, sometimes mummies get sick when they have babies, and it can take a while to get better.' 'How long is a while?' asked Sally. 'I don't know how long it will take, but I do know that she will get better again' said Rose. Sally frowned at Rose but Rose gave her a friendly smile. She told Sally and her dad that she would come back again next week.

Sally went back to her room, picked up her teddy bear and squeezed him tightly. A tear ran down her cheek. Her Dad came in and sat next to her on the bed. 'What's wrong Sally' he asked. Sally said 'I don't understand why mummy is sick…is it my fault daddy?' Her dad shook his head. 'It isn't anybody's fault. Do you remember when you had the chicken pox?' Sally nodded. 'That wasn't anybody's fault was it?' he said. Sally's voice quivered as she asked 'does mummy still love me?' Her dad wrapped his arms around her and whispered gently, 'Of course Sally, of course she loves you, and so do I. You were our first baby, and you will always be special to us, no one can replace you.' 'Then why wont she play with me anymore?' asked Sally. 'She keeps telling me to go away and she is always crying and yelling'. Another tear dropped from Sally's cheek. Her dad wiped it away and said quietly, 'When you are feeling sick Sally what do you do'. Suddenly, Sally grinned. 'I get grumpy and yell and then I cry because I feel so yucky. Mummy must be feeling yucky too'. Sally smiled and hugged her dad tightly.

Sally couldn't sleep. She stared out at the stars and thought about Ben, her Dad and her Mum. Sally thought about the new play group that she had been going to with her mum and Ben. Sally liked it because there were lots of children to play with and her mum liked it because she could meet other mums that weren't feeling well. Sally thought about her mum's new doctor whom she liked because she gave Sally stamps on the hand when they went there each week. The doctor gave Sally's mother some special medicine that was going to help her get better. Rose the nurse was visiting every week too. Sometimes Sally's mother cried when she spoke to Rose, but she told Sally that Rose was helping her to feel much better. Sally heard her mum laughing yesterday as she played with Ben on the floor. After dinner, Sally and her mum coloured in together and they did a drawing, which her mum stuck up on the fridge.

The door to Sally's room opened and her mother walked in. She sat down next to Sally and smiled as she looked out at the stars. She put her arm around her and whispered, 'choose a star Sally and make a wish.' Sally looked at her mother and smiled. 'Are you better now Mummy' she asked. 'Almost' said her mother. 'Then my wish has already come true mummy'. They sang 'twinkle twinkle little star' together and then her mother tucked her into bed, turned out the light, and Sally fell fast asleep.

Contacts page
Telephone numbers for Australian postnatal depression support groups and services.

QLD

PND SUPPORT GROUP ASSOCIATION —
PO Box 800 Springwood QLD 4127
Telephone Mobiles 015 119 061 or
041 763 2844

PND SUPPORT GROUP —
PO Box 268N
Cairns QLD
Telephone 07 4050 3100

NSW

PERSONAL SUPPORT NETWORK (SYDNEY)
108 Francis St
Leichhardt NSW 2040
Telephone 02 9540 5195
            02 9829 1103

MORUYA FAMILY SUPPORT SERVICE
(POSTCODE) 4414 2907

TAS

WALKER HOUSE PARENTING CENTRE
MASK (PND SUPPORT GROUP)
17a Walkers Avenue
Newnham TAS 7248
Telephone 03 6326 6188

THE PARENTING CENTRE
232 Newtown Road
Newtown TAS 7008
03 6233 2700

SA

OPND (OVERCOMING POSTNATAL
DEPRESSION)
08 8376 6772

Helen Mayo House
PO Box 17
Eastwood SA 5063
08 8303 1183

QUEEN ELIZABETH HOSPITAL
Woodville Road, Woodville SA
Social Worker
08 8222 6000

WA

METROPOLITAN SERVICES OFFERING PND
GROUPS:
Armadale —
08 9497 1413

Atwell Community Health —
08 9414 6011

Communicare Cannington —
08 9451 9777

Fremantle Women's Health Centre —
08 9430 4545

Granny Speirs Community House —
08 9401 7021

Gosnell's Women Health Care Place —
08 9490 2258

Ishar: Mulitcultural Women's Health
(Mirrabooka) — 08 9345 5335

Lockridge Community Health —
08 9279 0100

Loftus PND Support Group —
08 9328 3098

Midland Women's Health Care Place —
08 9250 2221

Northbridge Women's Health Care House —
08 9227 8122

Ngala (Kensington) —
08 9367 7855

Rockingham Community Health —
08 9527 8221

SELF HELP
POSTNATAL DEPRESSION SUPPORT
ASSOCIATION — 08 9340 1622

NT

PND SUPPORT GROUP (DARWIN)
29 Cardo Crt
Ludmilla NT 0820

ACT

ACT POSTNATAL DEPRESSION SUPPORT GROUP
Admin Line: 02 6286 4082
Fax: 02 6286 4083
PO Box 366
Curtin ACT 2605

www.ingramcontent.com/pod-product-compliance
Lightning Source LLC
Chambersburg PA
CBHW041101050426
42334CB00063B/3282